Photoshop

Davinder Singh Minhas

RISING SUN

RISING SUN
an imprint of
New Dawn Press

NEW DAWN PRESS GROUP
New Dawn Press, Inc., 244 South Randall Rd # 90, Elgin, IL 60123
e-mail: sales@newdawnpress.com
New Dawn Press, 2 Tintern Close, Slough, Berkshire, SL1-2TB, UK
e-mail: ndpuk@newdawnpress.com
         sterlingdis@yahoo.co.uk

New Dawn Press (An Imprint of Sterling Publishers (P) Ltd.)

A-59, Okhla Industrial Area, Phase-II, New Delhi-110020
e-mail: sterlingpublishers@touchtelindia.net
         Ghai@nde.vsnl.net.in

Printed at Sterling Publishers (P) Ltd., New Delhi-110020.

Contents

Contents

1. Introduction

Photoshop is an image editing software for the Macintosh and Windows from Adobe Corporation that allows you to create, modify, combine and optimize digital images. It contains a large variety of image editing features, one of its most powerful capabilities is *Filters*. Photoshop creates sophisticated images for both print and the Web.

You can apply colors or patterns to your images after selecting its pixels by using Photoshop's *Paintbrush*, *Airbrush*, *and Pencil* tools. You can also fill the arrows of your selections with solid or semitransparent colors.

You can brighten, darken, and change the hue (shade) of colors in parts of your image with Photoshop's *Dodge*, *Burn*, and similar tools. Photoshop's effects let you easily add *Drop shadows*, *3D shading*, and other styles to your images. You can also perform complex color manipulations or distortions with the help of Photoshop filters.

After you edit your work, you can use your images in a variety of ways. Photoshop lets you print your images, save them in a format suitable for use on a Web page, or prepare them for use in a page-layout program.

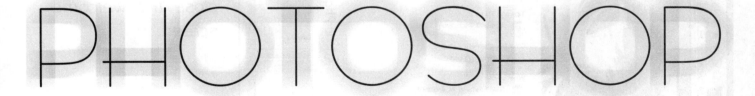

Starting Photoshop

You can start Photoshop on your PC and begin creating and editing digital images.

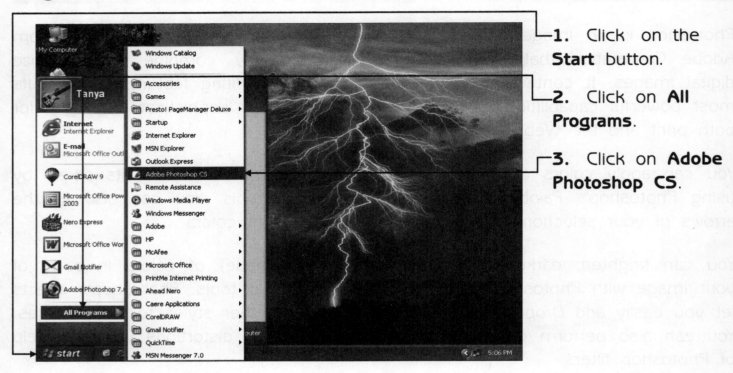

1. Click on the **Start** button.

2. Click on **All Programs**.

3. Click on **Adobe Photoshop CS**.

Photoshop appears on your screen.

*If the **Welcome Screen** appears, click on **Close** button to close the welcome screen.*

The Photoshop Workspace

To open and edit your images in Photoshop, you can use a combination of tools, menu commands, and palette-based features.

Menu Bar

Photoshop's commands are displayed in the Menu Bar.

Option Bar

Option bar displays controls that let you customize the selected tool in the toolbox.

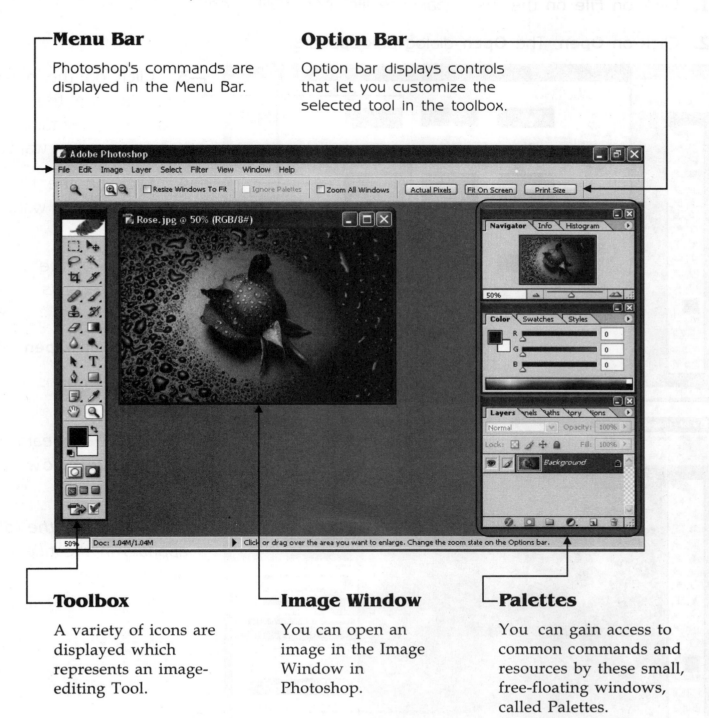

Toolbox

A variety of icons are displayed which represents an image-editing Tool.

Image Window

You can open an image in the Image Window in Photoshop.

Palettes

You can gain access to common commands and resources by these small, free-floating windows, called Palettes.

Opening an Image

You can open an existing image file in Photoshop.

1. Click on **File** on the menu bar. The file menu will open.

2. Click on **Open**. The **Open** dialog box appears.

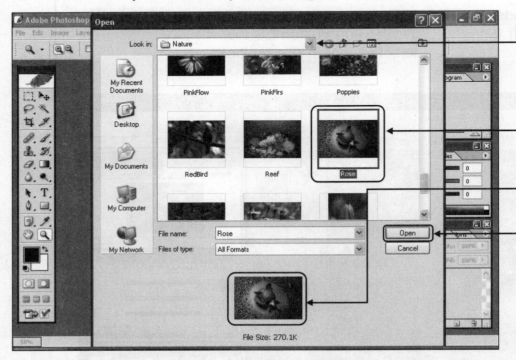

3. Click on the down arrow to see the folder that contains the image you want.

4. Click on the file name that you want to open.

A preview of the desired image is displayed.

5. Click on **Open**.

The image opens in Photoshop.

The image appears in a new window of Photoshop.

The name of the file appears in the title bar of the image.

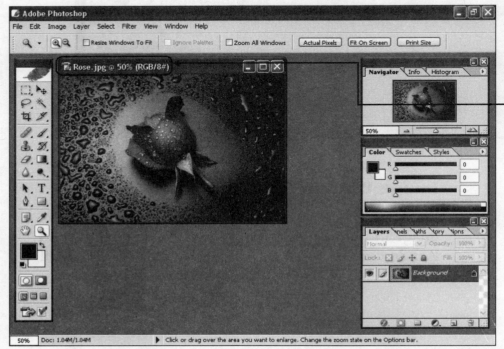

Creating an Image Window

By creating a blank image window, you can start working on Photoshop.

1. Click on **File** from the menu bar. The file menu will open.

2. Click on **New** from the menu bar. The **New** dialog box appears.

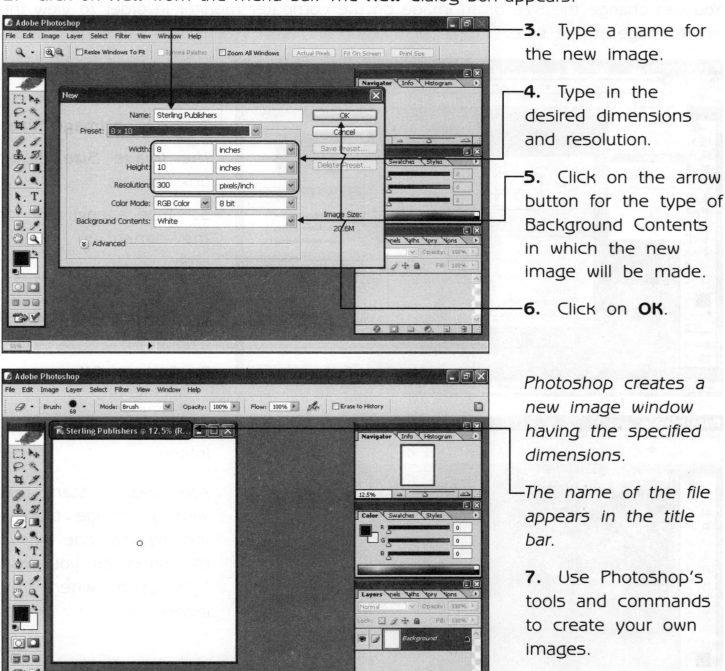

3. Type a name for the new image.

4. Type in the desired dimensions and resolution.

5. Click on the arrow button for the type of Background Contents in which the new image will be made.

6. Click on **OK**.

Photoshop creates a new image window having the specified dimensions.

The name of the file appears in the title bar.

7. Use Photoshop's tools and commands to create your own images.

2. Size of an Image

Changing the On-screen Size of an Image

You can change the size of an image on the computer monitor in order to view the entire image at one time.

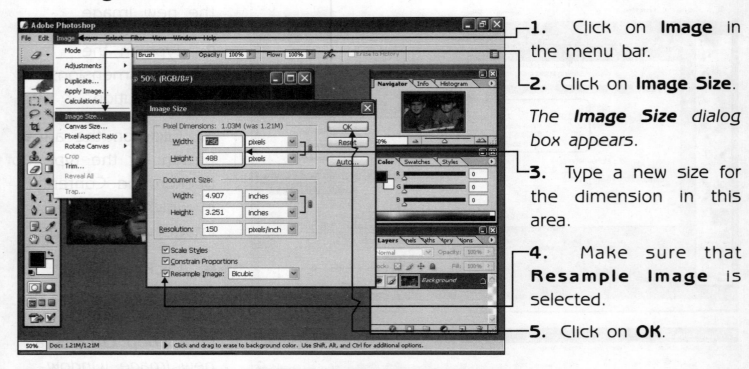

1. Click on **Image** in the menu bar.

2. Click on **Image Size**.

   *The **Image Size** dialog box appears.*

3. Type a new size for the dimension in this area.

4. Make sure that **Resample Image** is selected.

5. Click on **OK**.

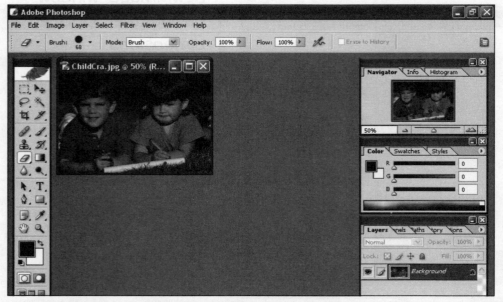

Photoshop resizes the image.

You should start this with an image that is too big than one that is too small as you lose less detail when you increase it.

Changing the Print Size of an Image

You can change the print size of an image in the following way:

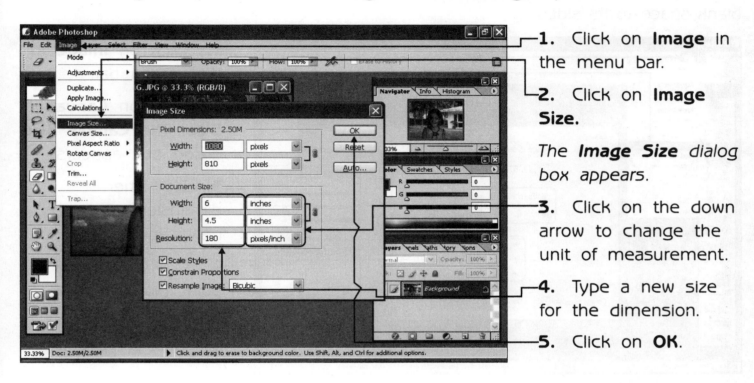

1. Click on **Image** in the menu bar.

2. Click on **Image Size.**

*The **Image Size** dialog box appears.*

3. Click on the down arrow to change the unit of measurement.

4. Type a new size for the dimension.

5. Click on **OK**.

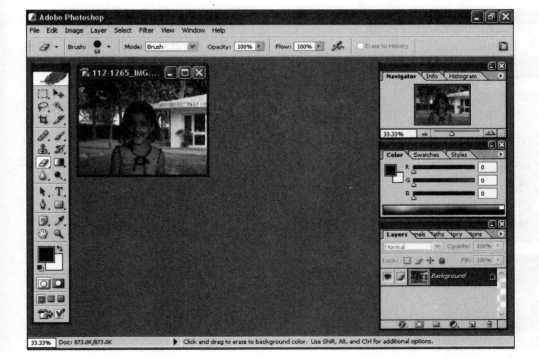

Photoshop resizes the image.

Changing the Canvas Size of an Image

The canvas size of an image can be changed to its rectangular shape or to add blank space to its sides.

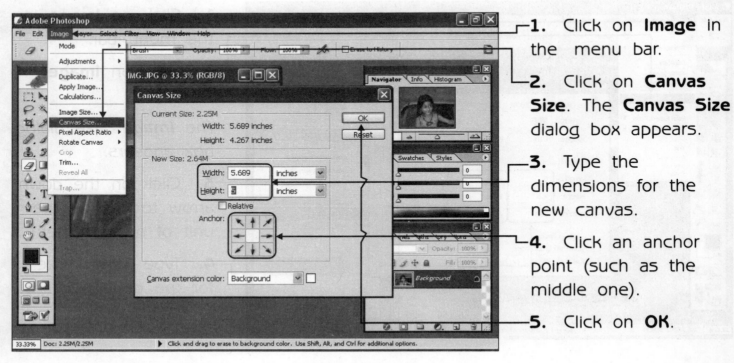

1. Click on **Image** in the menu bar.

2. Click on **Canvas Size**. The **Canvas Size** dialog box appears.

3. Type the dimensions for the new canvas.

4. Click an anchor point (such as the middle one).

5. Click on **OK**.

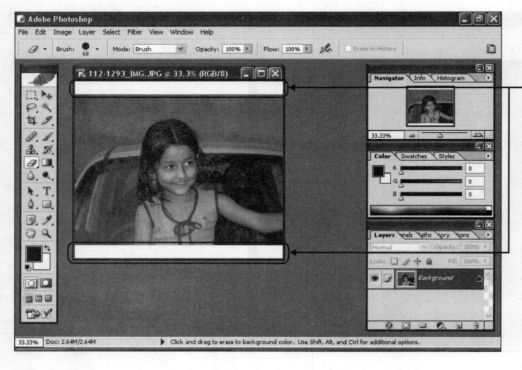

Photoshop changes the canvas size of the image.

The canvas changes equally on opposite sides because you have selected the middle anchor point.

Cropping the Image

To change the size of an image, **Crop Tool** can be used.

1. Click on the **Crop Tool** [⧆].

2. Click and drag to select the area of the image you want to keep.

3. You can click and drag the sides and corner handles to adjust the size of the cropping boundary.

4. Click on the **right button** or press the **Enter** key on the keyboard.

*Press **Esc** button on the keyboard to exit from the cropping process.*

Photoshop crops the image, deleting the pixels outside the cropping boundary.

3. Basic Tools

Zoom Tool

With the help of the Zoom tool, you can change the magnification of an image.

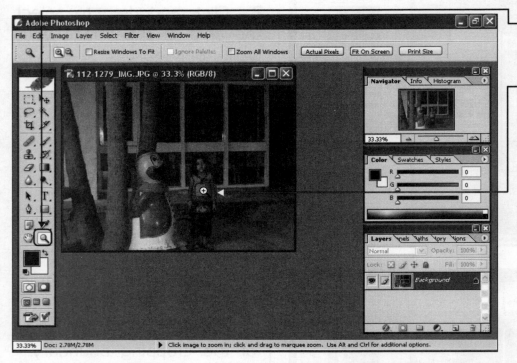

1. Click on the **Zoom Tool** ( ).

2. Click on the image that you want to magnify.

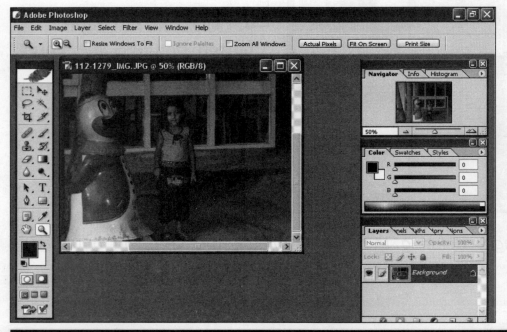

Photoshop increases the magnification of the image.

*After clicking on the Zoom tool ( ), press and hold the **Alt** key on the keyboard and click on the image to **decrease** the magnification.*

Changing Screen Modes

You can switch the screen mode to change the look of your work space on-screen.

Switch to Full Screen with Menu

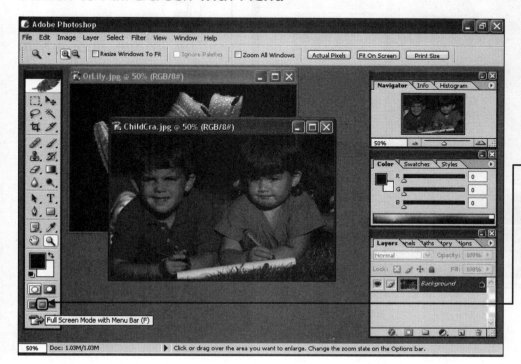

In standard screen mode, you can see multiple images at once, each in a different window.

1. Click on the **Full Screen Mode with Menu Bar** button ( ).

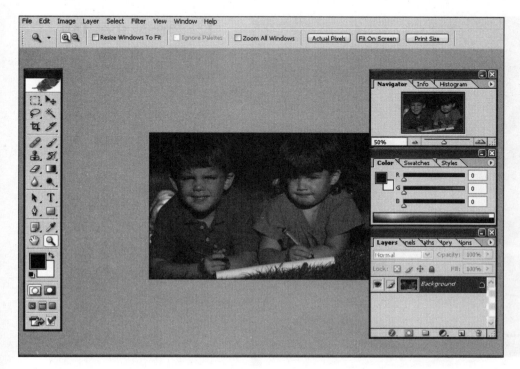

Photoshop puts the current image window in the center of a blank, full-screen canvas with the menu options at the top of the screen.

Switch to Full Screen

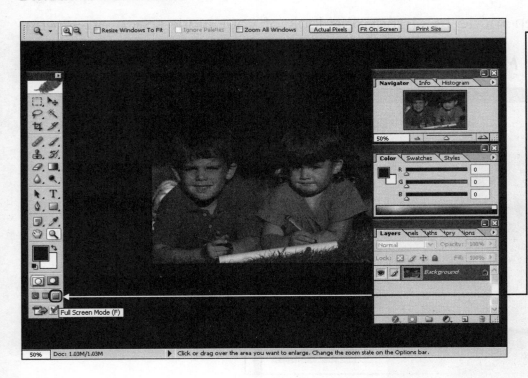

1. Click on the **Full Screen Mode** button ( ).

The image appears in full screen without the menu options.

Close Toolbox and Palette

1. Press the **Tab** button on the keyboard.

*Photoshop closes all the **toolboxes** and **palettes**.*

2. Now press the **Tab** button again on the keyboard to view the toolbox and palettes.

Selecting with Marquee Tools

Marquee tools are used to select a rectangular or elliptical area of your image. You can move, delete, or stylize the selected area using other Photoshop commands.

Rectangular Marquee Tool

1. Click on the **Rectangular Marquee Tool** [ ].

2. Click and drag diagonally inside the image window.

Elliptical Marquee Tool

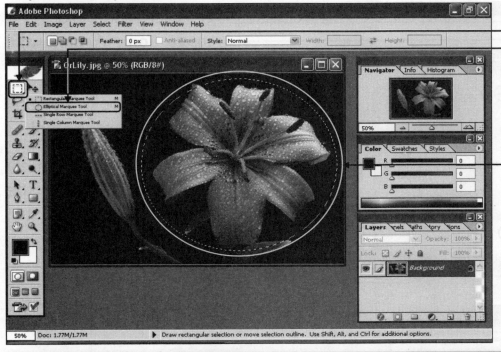

1. Click and hold **Rectangular Marquee Tool**. A **box** will appear.

2. In the box, select **Elliptical Marquee Tool**.

3. Click and drag diagonally inside the image window.

You can deselect a selection by clicking on **Select** *in the menu bar and then click on* **Deselect***.*

Selecting with Lasso Tool

With the help of **Lasso Tool**, you can create oddly shaped selections.

Regular Lasso Tool

1. Click on the **Lasso Tool**.

2. Click and drag with your cursor to make a selection.

3. Drag to the beginning point and release the mouse button to complete the selection.

Polygonal Lasso Tool

1. Click and hold **Lasso Tool**. A **box** will appear.

2. In the box, select **Polygonal Lasso Tool**.

3. Click multiple times along the border of the area you would like to select.

4. To complete the selection, click on the starting point.

Magnetic Lasso Tool

Magnetic Lasso Tool is used to select elements of your image that have well defined edges.

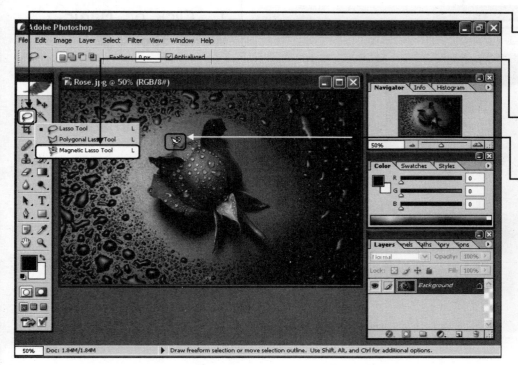

1. Click and hold **Lasso Tool**. A **box** will appear.

2. In the box, select **Magnetic Lasso Tool**.

3. Click on the edge of the element you want to select, to create the beginning anchor point.

4. Drag your cursor along the edge of the element. Magnetic Lasso snaps on to the edge of the element as you drag.

You can click to add anchor points as you go along, to guide the lasso.

5. Click on the beginning anchor point to finish your selection.

Selecting with Magic Wand Tool

Groups of similarly colored pixels can be selected with the use of **Magic Wand Tool**.

1. Click on **Magic Wand Tool** [⚲].

2. Click on the area you want to select inside the image.

Photoshop selects the pixel you clicked, and any similarly colored pixels near it.

Delete selected pixels

1. Press the **Delete** key on the keyboard to delete the selected pixels.

The pixels are replaced with the background color (in this case, white).

Photoshop

Moving the Selection

With the help of **Move Tool**, you can move a selection which lets you rearrange the elements of your image.

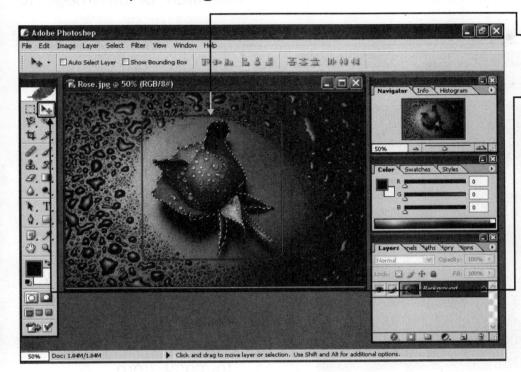

1. Make a selection with any of the selection tools.

2. Click on **Move Tool** [ ].

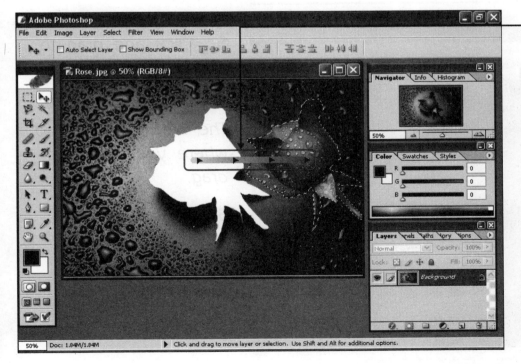

3. Click inside the selection and drag.

The area appears where the selection used to be filled with the current background color.

White is the default background color.

21

Rubber Stamp Tool

You can clean up small flaws or erase elements in your image with the help of **Rubber Stamp Tool**. The tool copies information from one area of an image to another.

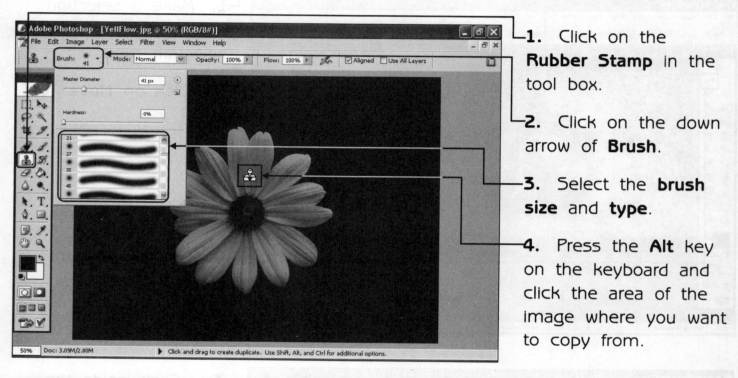

1. Click on the **Rubber Stamp** in the tool box.

2. Click on the down arrow of **Brush**.

3. Select the **brush size** and **type**.

4. Press the **Alt** key on the keyboard and click the area of the image where you want to copy from.

5. Click and drag to apply the rubber stamp.

The area is copied to where you click and drag.

6. Click and drag repeatedly over the area to achieve the desired effect.

4. Color Modes

RGB Mode

RGB is the most common mode for working with color images in Photoshop.

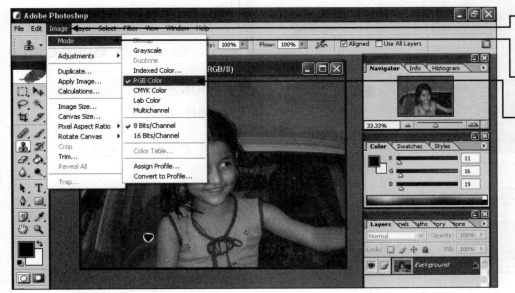

1. Click on **Image** in the menu bar.

2. Click on **Mode**.

3. Click on **RGB Color**.

RGB is displayed in the title bar of the image.

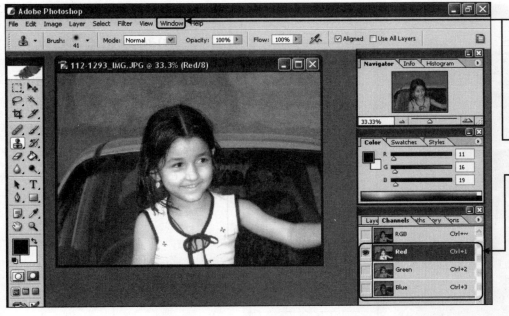

4. To view the different color components of an RGB image, click on **Window**.

5. Click on **Channels**.

6. Click on any channel (Red, Green or Blue).

A grayscale version of the image displays the amount of channels the image contains.

For example when you choose the red channel, the lighter areas shows lot of red; darker areas shows very little red.

Drag and Drop Series

Converting Color Images to Grayscale

To remove the color from your image, you can convert it to grayscale mode.

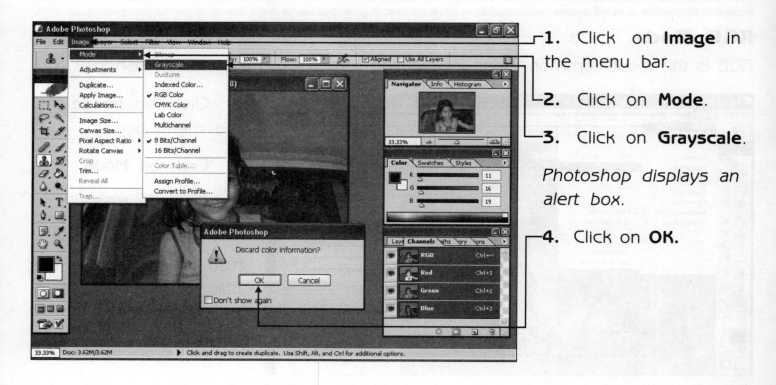

1. Click on **Image** in the menu bar.

2. Click on **Mode**.

3. Click on **Grayscale**.

Photoshop displays an alert box.

4. Click on **OK.**

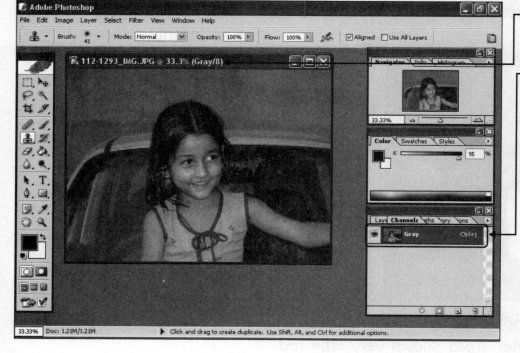

Gray is displayed in the image title bar.

Grayscale images have a single channel, that is why grayscale image files take up less space than RGB images.

Foreground and Background Colors

A foreground color and a background color can be selected by you to work in Photoshop.

Foreground Color

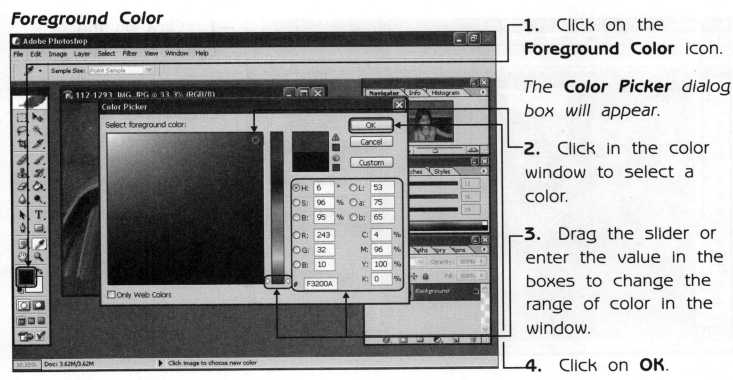

1. Click on the **Foreground Color** icon.

*The **Color Picker** dialog box will appear.*

2. Click in the color window to select a color.

3. Drag the slider or enter the value in the boxes to change the range of color in the window.

4. Click on **OK**.

Background Color

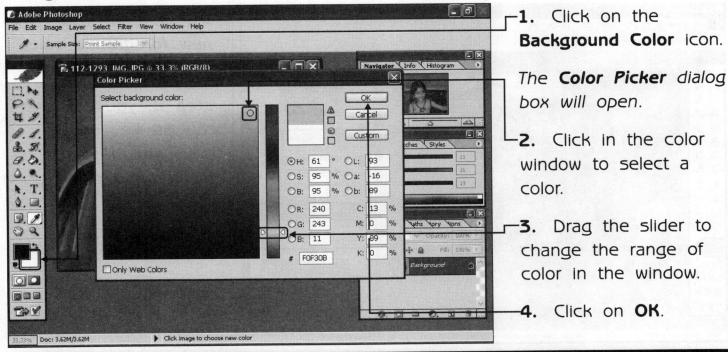

1. Click on the **Background Color** icon.

*The **Color Picker** dialog box will open.*

2. Click in the color window to select a color.

3. Drag the slider to change the range of color in the window.

4. Click on **OK**.

Selecting Color using Eyedropper Tool

You can select a color from an open image with the Eyedropper tool. This tool enables you to paint using a color already present in your image.

1. Click on the **Eyedropper Tool [✎]**.

2. Place the Eyedropper tool over an open image and click to select the color under Eyedropper tool's tip.

*The color becomes the new **foreground** color.*

*As you perform in **step 2**, you can press the **Alt** key on the keyboard to select the **background** color too.*

Using Paintbrush Tool

You can use the **Paintbrush Tool** to add color to your image.

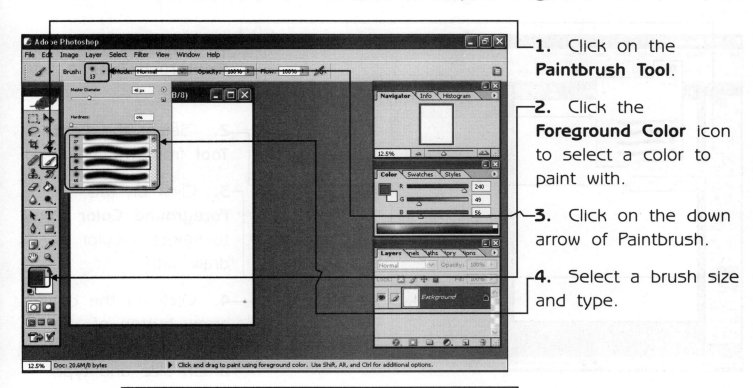

1. Click on the **Paintbrush Tool**.

2. Click the **Foreground Color** icon to select a color to paint with.

3. Click on the down arrow of Paintbrush.

4. Select a brush size and type.

5. Click and drag to apply the foreground color to the image.

6. Type the percentage value to change the opacity of the brush strokes.

7. Click and drag to apply the semi-transparent paintbrush.

Using Pencil Tool

Pencil Tool is used to draw straight lines of color.

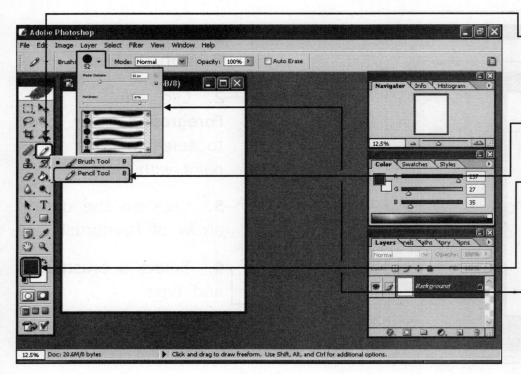

1. Click and hold the **Paintbrush Tool**. A box appears.

2. Select the **Pencil Tool** from the box.

3. Click on the **Foreground Color** icon to select a color to draw with

4. Click on the down arrow button of Paintbrush and select a brush size and type.

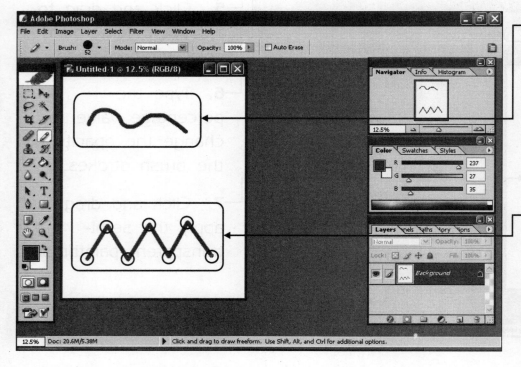

5. Click and drag to apply the foreground color to the image.

DRAW STRAIGHT LINES

6. Press and hold **Shift**.

7. Click on several places inside your image, without dragging.

Photoshop draws straight lines.

Using Paint Bucket Tool

An area can be filled in your image with solid color using the **Paint Bucket Tool**.

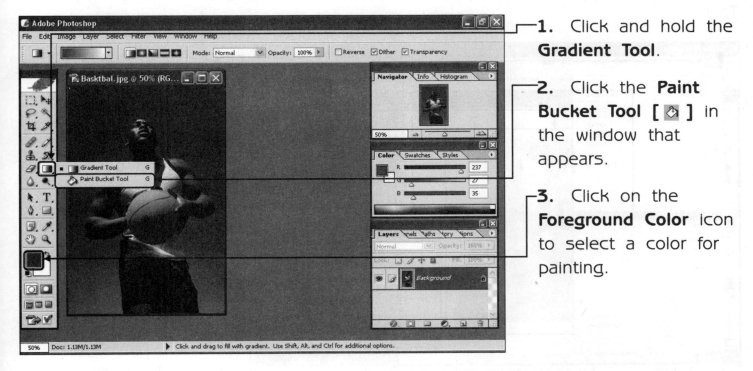

1. Click and hold the **Gradient Tool**.

2. Click the **Paint Bucket Tool [◊]** in the window that appears.

3. Click on the **Foreground Color** icon to select a color for painting.

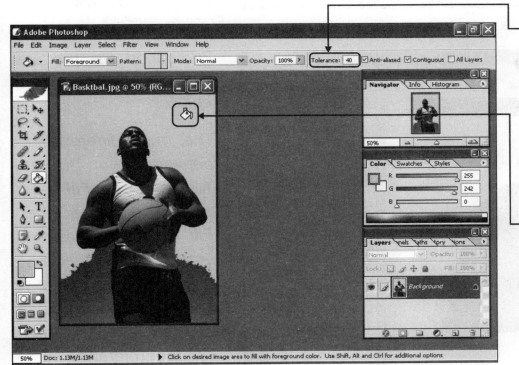

4. Type a **Tolerance value** from 0 to 255.

*The **Tolerance value** determines what range of colors the paint bucket affects in the image when applied.*

5. Click inside the image.

Photoshop fills an area of image with the foreground color.

The Paint Bucket Tool affects adjacent pixels in the image.

Fill In the Selection

Fill command is used to fill a selection. It is an alternative to the Paint Bucket Tool.

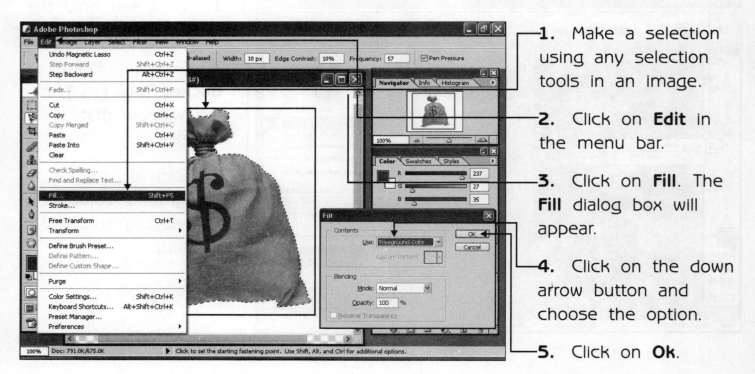

1. Make a selection using any selection tools in an image.

2. Click on **Edit** in the menu bar.

3. Click on **Fill**. The **Fill** dialog box will appear.

4. Click on the down arrow button and choose the option.

5. Click on **Ok**.

Photoshop fills the area with the foreground color.

*The main difference between Paint Bucket Tool and the **Fill** command is that the **Fill** command fills the entire selected area with the foreground color, not just adjacent pixels based on the tolerance value.*

5. Color Adjustments

Brightness and Contrast

You can adjust the Brightness and Contrast of your image.

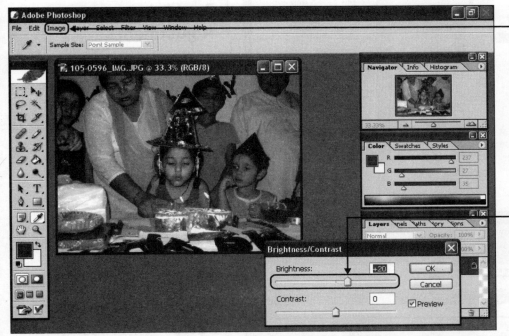

1. Click on **Image** in the menu bar.

2. Click on **Adjustments**.

3. Click on **Brightness/Contrast**.

   A dialog box appears.

4. To lighten the image, click and drag the **Brightness:** slider to the right, or darken the image by dragging it to the left.

5. To increase the contrast, click and drag the **Contrast:** slider to the right, or to decrease contrast, drag it to the left.

6. Click on **OK**.

31

Color Balance

To change the amount of specific colors in your image, you can use the Color Balance command.

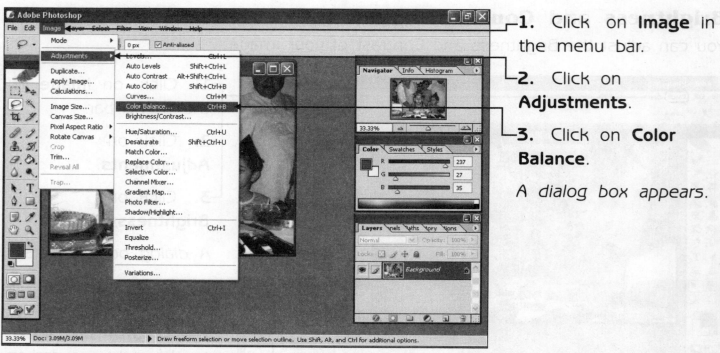

1. Click on **Image** in the menu bar.

2. Click on **Adjustments**.

3. Click on **Color Balance**.

   A dialog box appears.

4. Select the radio button of tones in the image that you want to affect.

5. Click and drag the color slider to adjust the color or type a number from -100 to 100 in the **Color Levels:** field.

6. Click on **OK**.

You can drag a slider towards red or magenta to add a warm effect to your image. To add a cool effect, you can drag the slider towards blue or cyan.

Color Variations

To make color adjustments in your image, you can get a user-friendly interface by **Variations** command.

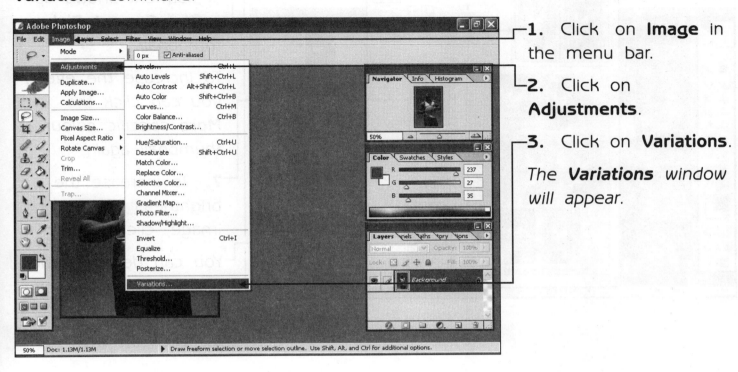

1. Click on **Image** in the menu bar.

2. Click on **Adjustments**.

3. Click on **Variations**.

   *The **Variations** window will appear.*

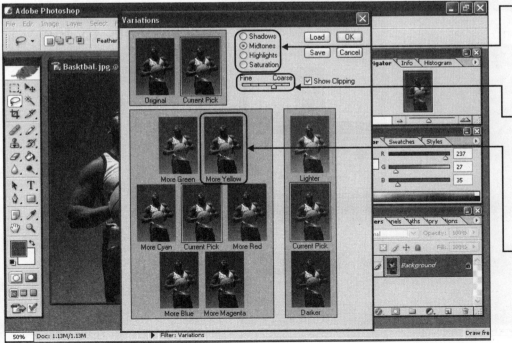

4. Click on the radio button to select the different tones in image.

5. Move the slider left to make Fine (small) adjustments or right to make Coarse (large) adjustments.

6. To add a color to your image, click one of the **More** specific color thumbnail visuals.

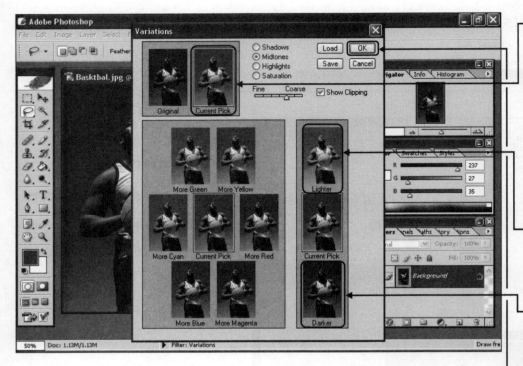

The result of the adjustment shows up in the **Current Pick** thumbnail.

To increase the effect, you can click the **More** *specific colour thumbnail again.*

7. To increase the brightness of the image, click **Lighter**.

You can decrease the brightness by clicking ***Darker***.

8. Click on **OK**.

Photoshop makes color adjustments to the image.

Using Dodge Effect

You can use the Dodge tool to lighten a specific area of an image. **Dodge** is a photographic term that describes the diffusing of light when developing a film negative.

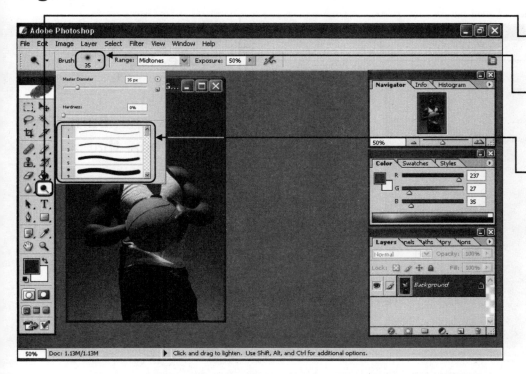

1. Click on the **Dodge Tool**.

2. Click on the down arrow button of **Brush:** menu.

3. Click the brush size and type that you would like to use.

4. You can also select the range of colors you want to affect.

5. Click and drag over the area that you want to lighten.

Using Burn Effect

You can use the Burn Tool to darken a specific area of an image. **Burn** is a photographic term that describes the focusing of light when developing a film negative.

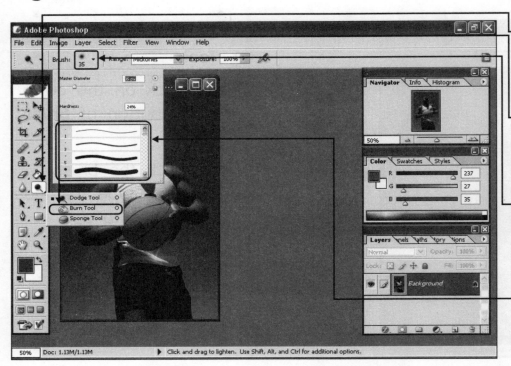

1. Click and hold the **Dodge Tool**. A box appears.

2. Click the **Burn Tool** in the box that appears.

3. Click on the down arrow button of **Brush:** menu.

4. Click the brush size and type that you would like to use.

5. You can also select the range of colors you want to affect.

6. Click and drag over the area that you want to darken.

6. Filters

Brush Strokes Using Crosshatch Filter

The **Crosshatch Filter** adds diagonal, overlapping brush-stroke effect to your image.

1. Click on **Filter**.

2. Click on **Brush Strokes**.

3. Click on **Crosshatch**.

A window appears displaying a preview of the filter's effect.

4. This area shows the thumbnails of selected filters. you can choose another filter style from this area.

5. Fine-tune the filter effects by adjusting the **Stroke Length**, **Sharpness**, and **Strength** values.

6. Click on **OK**.

Photoshop applies the filter to the image.

Distort Filter Using Spherize Filter

The **Spherize Filter** produces a fun-house effect because it can stretch and squeeze areas of your image.

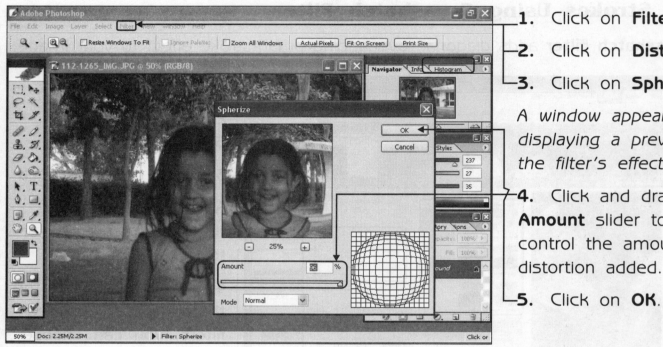

1. Click on **Filter**.

2. Click on **Distort**.

3. Click on **Spherize**.

   A window appears displaying a preview of the filter's effect.

4. Click and drag the **Amount** slider to control the amount of distortion added.

5. Click on **OK**.

Photoshop applies the filter to the image.

Render Filter Using Lighting Effects Filter

The **Lighting Effects Filter** lets you add spotlight and other lighting enhancements.

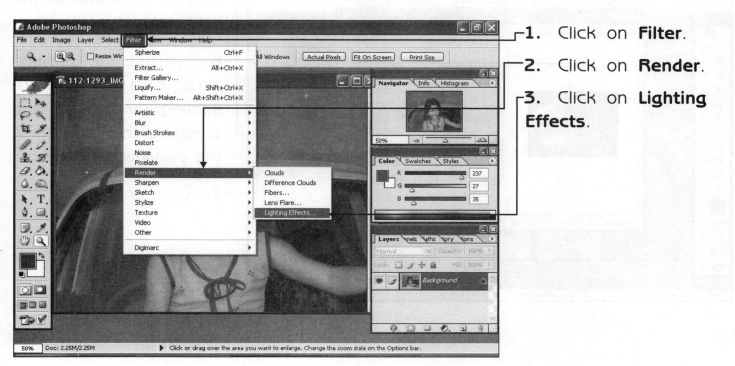

1. Click on **Filter**.

2. Click on **Render**.

3. Click on **Lighting Effects**.

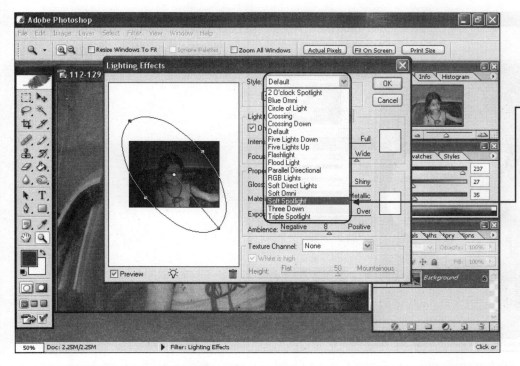

A window appears displaying a preview of the filter's effect.

4. Click on the down arrow button of **Style:** and choose a lighting style.

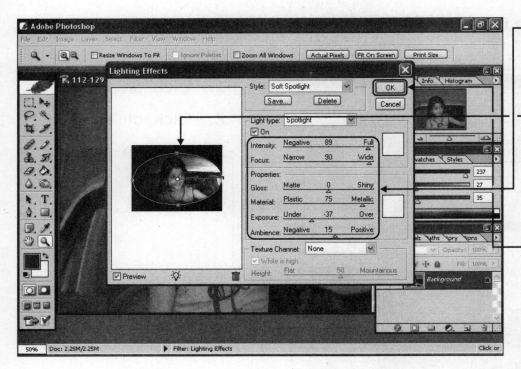

5. Click and drag the sliders to control the light intensity.

6. Adjust the position and shape of the lighting by clicking and dragging the handles in the preview window.

7. Click on **OK**.

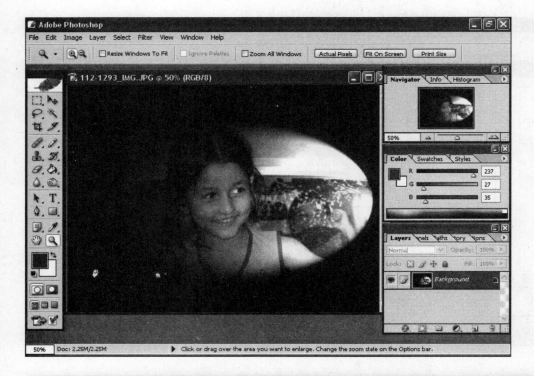

Photoshop applies the filter to the image.